著名油画家侯一民先生为本书题写书名

图书在版编目(CIP)数据

　　大漠奇石瑰宝／石心 编著. —北京：华艺出版社，
2008.7

　　ISBN 978-7-80142-909-4

　　Ⅰ.大… Ⅱ.石… Ⅲ.奇石—内蒙古-图集 Ⅳ.G894-64

　　中国版本图书馆CIP数据核字（2008）第099414号

书　　名：大漠奇石瑰宝
作　　者：石　心
策　　划：魏进学　骆彦卿
责任编辑：郑治清
摄　　影：赵立云
装帧设计：赵立云
版式设计：北京春晓伟业图书发行有限公司
篆　　刻：李长贵
出版发行：华艺出版社
印　　刷：精美彩色印刷有限公司
版　　次：2008年8月第1版　 2008年8月第1次印刷
开　　本：889×1194　 1/16　 印张：14.5
定　　价：320.00元

地　　址：北京北四环中路229号海泰大厦10层　　邮　　编：100083
电　　话：010-82885151-222　　 82855023　　 E－mail：fujiang_song18@sina.com

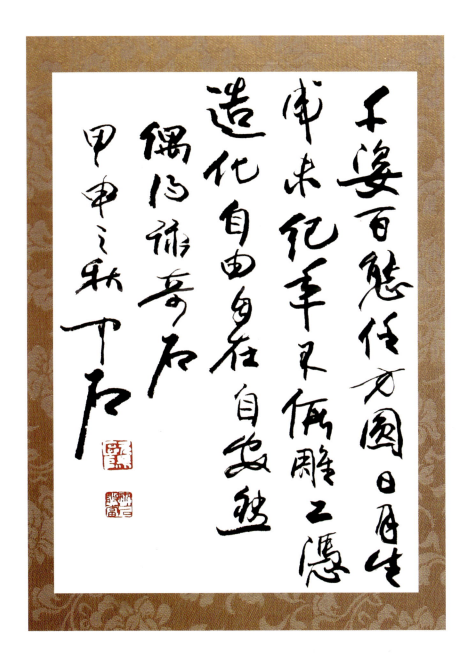

千姿百态任方圆日月生

佛来纪手又俩雕工凭

造化自由多在自安然

偶得述奇石

甲申之秋中石

著名书法家欧阳中石先生题词

大漠奇石瑰宝
Desert Rare Stone Museum Treasures

4

古石生靈草

長松棲異禽

著名奇石收藏家、大漠奇石馆馆长魏进学题词

拜石图：著名油画家侯一民

6

点石成金图：著名国画家纪则夫

中国北京昌平大漠奇石馆
China Beijing Changping Desert Rare Stone Museum

通向大漠奇石馆的交通指示路牌
Transportation Signpost

大漠奇石馆被北京市昌平区旅游局、昌平区科协授予
"青少年旅游科普教育基地"
Desert Rare Stone Museum was awarded by the
government as the Youth Tourism & Popular
Science Education Base

大漠奇石馆
Desert Rare Stone Museum Treasures

Desert Rare Stone Museum Treasures

展室内景
Desert Rare Stone Museum
Exhibition Hall

展室内景
Desert Rare Stone Museum
Exhibition Hall

展室外景
Desert Rare Stone Museum
Exterior Scene

坚如大漠石的精神
（代序）

　　借着在北京昌平区旅游企业创建青少年旅游科普教育基地的机会，让我走进了位于流村镇古将村的大漠奇石馆，使我有幸结识了大漠奇石收藏家魏进学先生。

　　走进奇石馆，映入眼帘的则是千姿百态、造型生动、变化万千的世间万象。蓝色的玛瑙、紫色的水晶、红绿碧玉、雪白的玉髓、黑色的玫瑰、棕色的集骨、五光十色……真是无奇不有，美妙绝伦。在这之前我从没有见过也没有听说过这么多好看的奇石，于是，我就有了想了解这些奇石，想了解魏先生其人的愿望。

　　1948年，魏进学先生出生在冀中平原上的河北蠡县，从学生时代，就对石头产生了浓厚的兴趣，几十年工作中，他当过兵，做过成功的企业家。十五年前，为了这个爱好，他毅然放弃了其他工作，走上了艰难的藏石之路。魏先生用四年时间四次深入内蒙古的巴彦淖尔盟、阿拉善盟一带，累计行程8000余公里，收集了近四十辆大卡车的奇石。环境的恶劣，路途的险阻，甚至是对生命极限的一次次挑战，都没能动摇他收集大漠奇石的信心和决心。他是用生命在谱写一段藏石的传奇文化。

　　正所谓石如其人，人若其石，大漠石的特点是硬、真、朴，搞不了假。魏先生何尝不是这种性格呢！记得在大漠奇石馆落成剪彩仪式上，朋友劝他换下满是泥土灰尘的衣服，他说："石头是自然的，我本人也就是这个模样，因为每天都要整理我的石头，拥抱我的石头。"

　　是啊！魏先生爱石如命，成为世间少有的"石痴"。整天和石头对话，就像生活中不可缺少的人生"伴侣"。我常和他开玩笑说，他本人就有着一张玛瑙脸，可以说石头就是他的"魂"，他把每一块石头常看成是一幅画、一首诗、一支歌。

　　当我们问到他，为什么要建馆，还要对游人开放？他说："独赏不如共赏，让大家都欣赏，大家的心情才能得到愉悦，不就更好吗？"

　　对于成长中的年轻一代，欣赏奇石又是一个很好的科普教育形式。它带来的不仅是视觉上的惊艳，还有对大自然鬼斧神工的慨叹，在丰富了知识的同时，又学习到其中所蕴含的奇石精神。从而更加热爱我们的家园，珍惜这带给我们神奇之旅的地球。正如魏先生建馆的初衷——"独乐乐，不如众乐乐！"既然如此，何乐而不为呢？！

北京市昌平区科学技术协会副主席

杨凤霞

2008年6月28日

大漠石馆藏
Desert Rare Stone Museum Treasures

Spirit as Hard as Han Stone
(Preface)

Taking the chance of setting up the Youth Tourism & Popular Science Education Base in tourism enterprises of Changping District, Beijing, I had an access to the Desert Rare Stone Museum in Gujiang Village, Liusha Town and got acquainted with Mr. Wei Jinxue, a collector of desert rare stones.

Stepping into the museum, I was fascinated with the various shapes, styles, forms and colors of rare stones, such as blue agate, purple crystal, read and green jasper, snow white chalcedony, black rose marble, brown jigu stone, etc. What a fabulous picture there! Before this visit I had never heard or seen such wonderful rare stones. Thus I came up with a desire to know more about them as well as Mr. Wei.

Mr. Wei Jinxue, born in Li County, Hebei Province of Jizhong Plain in 1948, developed an interest in stones when he was a student. During decades of working experience, he was ever an army soldier and then a successful entrepreneur. In the pursuit of this hobby, he gave up career 15 years ago and began to collect rare stones. He spent 4 years' time paying four in-depth visits to Bayannaoer League and Alasan League of Inner Mogolia, totally covering over 8,000 kilometers and collecting nearly 40 trucks of rare stones. Harsh environment, dangerous road, or even severe challenges to the limit of life could not conquer his confidence and great determination. He has been composing a legend history of rare stones with his own life.

It is said that collectors and their stones interact. The characteristics of desert stones are hard, genuine and simple, which exactly summarizes Mr. Wei's personality. On the ribbon-cutting ceremony of Desert Rare Stone Museum, though Mr. Wei's friends tried to persuade him to change his dusty clothes, he refused, saying, "The stones are natural and so am I. I am what I look right now, for I have to deal with my stones every day."

Mr. Wei values stones as his own life and becomes a stone addict rarely seen in this world.

He talks with the stones as if they are integral life companion of his. I used to joke with him that he has a face looking like agate. Stone is simply his soul and he regards every single piece as a painting, a poem or a song.

When we asked him why he set up the museum and allowed visitors to access, he answered, "To appreciate beauty by oneself is not as good as to share beauty with others. Isn't it a better idea to bring happiness to others?"

For the younger generation, appreciating rare stones is also a good way to spread popular science education, which not only amazes their eyes with nature's marvels, but enriches their knowledge and enables them to exploit the included spirit of rare stones as well. Thus they will love our home more, and better cherish the globe where they live. Just as Mr. Wei's original intention indicated, "Rather than oneself happy, why not make everyone happy?" Doesn't that make more sense?

Beijing Changping Science technigue association Vice-chairman
Yang Feng Xia
2008.6.28

10

目录

象形石

大漠奇石瑰宝
Desert Rare Stone Museum Treasures

12

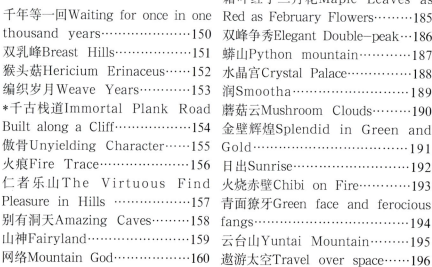

景观 静物石

大漠奇石的成因、欣赏与收藏

　　随着国内外收藏热的不断升温，奇石收藏也是异军突起，在国际拍品中也常见奇石的身影。在我国和亚太地区，大漠奇石收藏在收藏界也似如一朵盛开的奇葩，日新月异！

　　亿万年前，由于内蒙、新疆独特的地质结构和地壳错位、变迁、火山爆发以及风吹、沙砾等原因，在浩浩大漠和苍苍戈壁，经严酷的大自然洗礼，在每块石头上都留下了岁月的精华，造就了数以万计美轮美奂的大漠精灵。人们赏之愉悦、如梦如幻、神韵无穷。在收藏界，人们给它起了几多很好听的名字：有人叫它大漠石，有人叫它戈壁石，有人叫它风砺石；也有人叫它风凌石。只有新疆统称它为大漠石。大漠奇石涵盖玛瑙、碧玉、玉髓、千层石、玄武岩、硅化木等，其多数是硅质类奇石，硬度在6.5—7.0度。

　　"石不能言最可人"，爱石藏石，既能满足人们崇尚自然、返璞归真的心态，陶冶情操和生活上得到高雅精神享受，又有收藏、观赏、科研、传世和日益显现的经济价值。在奇石收藏中，判断一方大漠奇石的好坏、有无收藏价值，要从它独具的特点中，着重看它的质地、形状、色彩和意境几方面因素。

　　质地：质地是指奇石的化学成份和物理性质，也是评定一方奇石价值的重要因素之一。一块硅质的玛瑙玉石与一块灰质、沙质岩的山石相比，就好似金子与铜之比，大漠奇石绝大部分品种质地为硅质。密度越大，质地纯者为上品。由于它硬度大、质地坚硬，人工不易打磨，即使有一点打磨或修整，人工痕迹也会一目了然，因此，做假、赝品对大漠石而言，难！

　　形状：形状对于一方奇石而言是衡量它是否有无收藏、观赏的重要标准之一。形态多姿、造型奇特、气势恢宏是大漠奇石的第二大特点。它的外形千姿百态，形象万千，天上、人间、人物、动物、鱼虫花鸟的造型在大漠奇石中应有尽有。造型奇特、叫人过目难忘的为精品，更上档次精品，不但形似而且神似，以至能达到逼真的程度。

　　颜色：颜色会使奇石增奇和宣染主题。色彩丰富、润泽是大漠奇石的第三大特点。由于大漠奇石含有不同的矿物成份，所以它有单色和复色之分，单色纯洁略显剔透，复色艳丽流光溢彩。更神奇的大漠奇石绝品，在它形似、神似的造型中，还能同时"克隆"出象形物的各部颜色，以神奇叫绝天下！

　　近年来，收藏上几件附有"黑里红"和"熟蟹红"色沙漠漆的大漠奇石，是个值得炫耀的话题。在此画册中，这样的沙漠漆比比皆是，可谓沙漠漆荟萃！

　　意境：意境对于一方奇石而言，似如人有无灵魂、精气神一样。一块好的大漠奇石，应该是越看越耐看，它意境之渊、神韵之美，会令人神驰意远，这也正是大漠奇石的第四大突出特点。由于大漠奇石生成年代久远，所处人烟稀少的大漠戈壁，亿万年中无人访扰，天时地利人和加之鬼斧神工的自然力量，使它形成了富有灵性、世间无奇不有、色彩丰富、千姿百态的形状。

　　大漠奇石，珠光宝气、流光溢彩！它是雄浑大漠、浩荡戈壁，在独特的地理环境和严酷的大自然洗礼下，被注入了大漠戈壁魂的大自然产物；它，历经磨难而坚韧、大雅大俗而超然；它，奇在鬼斧神工、贵在天然造化、美在千姿百态、妙在举世无双。大漠奇石，奇石收藏者的最爱！

Formation Cause, Appreciation & Collection
of Desert Rare Stones

As collection is becoming more and more popular both home and abroad, the collection of rare stones appears as a new force that suddenly arises. You can even see them among international auction articles. In our country as well as Asia-pacific region, desert rare stones are also like a fantastic flower full in blossom and growing with time in the collection circle.

Hundreds of millions of years ago, due to the unique geometrical structure and some other causes such as lithosphere dislocation, transition, volcanic eruption, wind blow, gravel, etc. in Inner Mongolia and Xinjiang, tens of thousands of marvelous desert "genii" came into being over the vast Gobi desert, with years' essence left on every single piece of stone through harsh natural development. People feel refreshed when appreciating them, as if they were in a dream full of lasting charm and appeal. In collection circle, they are favorably named as desert stones, or Gobi stones, or fengli stones, or fengling stones. Only in Xinjiang they have one unified name, desert stones. Generally desert rare stones include agate, jasper, chalcedony, qianceng stone, basalt, silicified wood, etc, most of which belong to siliceous category, with hardness ranging from 6.5 to 7.0 degrees.

"The stone that cannot speak deserves utmost love from people". To love and collect stones satisfies people's demand to admire nature and return to the original simple past, nurtures people's sentiment with elegant spiritual enjoyment, and brings increasingly obvious economic value in terms of collection, appreciation, scientific research and inheritage. In rare stone collection, to tell a desert rare stone good from bad, with or without collecting value, largely depends on several factors out of its unique features, i.e. texture, shape, color and artistic conception.

14

Substance: substance refers to the chemical composition and physical property of rare stones. It serves as one of the essential factors to judge the value of rare stone. Comparing an agate of silicon substance with a stone of gravel or sand substance, is just like comparing gold with bronze. Desert rare stones are mostly of silicon substance. Top grade is always with greater density and purer substance. As it is hard, difficult to grind or finish, even a little bit of grinding or trimming would make labor traces clear at a glance. Thus it is more difficult to cheat on desert stones.

Shape: shape is one of the essential standards to judge a rare stone if it is of collection or appreciation value. Various forms, odd shapes and imposing manner are the second outstanding feature of Desert rare stones. A rare stone may have every shape or image that one expects to find, like the heaven and the world, people, animals, fish, insects, flowers and birds, etc. Those in odd shape that impress people at a glance are exquisite stones, while others with similarity in both shape and spirit to a vivid degree are of even higher rank.

Color: color can add oddness to rare stones and exaggerate the theme. Rich in color and glitter is the third feature of desert rare stones. Due to different mineral composition they have, the color includes single shade and compound shade. Single shade looks pure and slightly transparent while compound shade has flowing colors and glitters. More amazing is the one which has similar shape and spirit and meanwhile "clones" exactly every color of different parts as the original.

In recent years, it became a topic worth showing off to collect several desert rare stones with "black and red" or "cooked crab red" desert paint. Such desert paints can be found everywhere in this album, which can be called a constellation of desert paints.

Artistic conception: conception is to a rare stone what soul or spirit is to a man. For a good desert rare stone, the longer you look at it, the more charm and appeal you'll find. Its broad artistic conception and wonderful verve makes you relax and think far beyond, which is said to be the fourth feature of desert rare stones. Long years of formation, special location in the Gobi desert with few human habitation, free from visits or disturbance throughout hundreds of millions of years, and influence from climate, geographic position, people's support plus great natural force, all of which enable the desert rare stone to form spiritual, odd, colorful and various shapes.

With flowing colors and glitters, desert rare stones are natural result embedded with Gobi spirit through all harsh and severe tests of nature in the unique geographic environment of Gobi desert. They become tough and resilient with all hardships, and detached with elegance and convention. Featuring in nature's creation and formation, various shapes, as well as unique conception, the desert rare stones are the most loved ones of extensive collectors.

象 形 石

Pictograph Stone Chapter

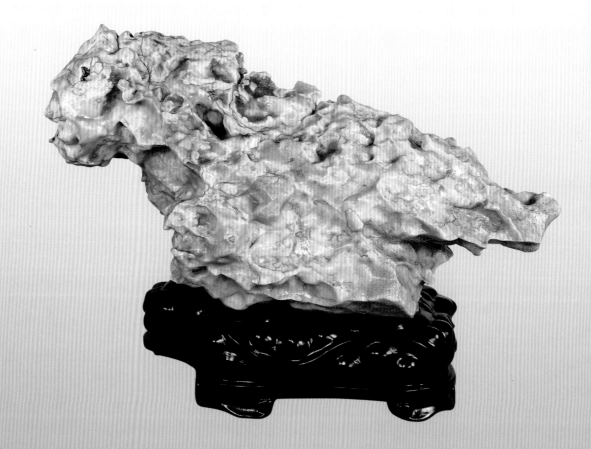

16

古龙（沙漠漆）
Ancient Dragon
玛瑙玉髓共生石
33×25×24cm

（背面）

猿人 <small>（沙漠漆）</small>

Ape Man

玛瑙玉髓共生石

35×21×16cm

（背面）

象形石

18

思之源 (沙漠漆)
Source of Thought
玉髓石
21×21×15cm

*岁月

Ages
三色玛瑙玉石
15×8×10cm
重整整1000克！神！

千古因缘和合生，　人类史前亿寿星。
娑婆世界凝满目，　慈悲老妪著永恒。

　　两亿年前火山爆发后天然逐渐形成的这尊人像石神品，它一问世就在国内外收藏界、赏石界引起了极大的轰动！超百家国内外电视、报纸、杂志、网站等媒体竟相报道。
老妪慈善、慈祥的面容，以及逼真的造型和传神的风采，使人们无不惊叹大自然造物的高超、神奇！当有人类时，《岁月》已是亿岁寿星了。老妪造像妙在自然，独具神韵。五官比例恰当，巧在天然色彩搭配贴切，与人的肤色、头发一样。千古因缘赋予此石的巨大魅力，有何种艺术品能与其媲美！

　　《岁月》的丰富内涵和苍天造化之奥秘，宛如一部天书、奥妙无穷。它被原故宫博物院副院长杨伯达等五位国家顶级宝玉石专家共同鉴评为具有极高的收藏、观赏、经济和科学研究价值，被收藏界和赏石界誉为 国际石坛的天然力作和举世无双的国宝！

宁夏邮政局、宁夏集邮公司和宁夏收藏家
协会共同制作发行的《岁月》邮票

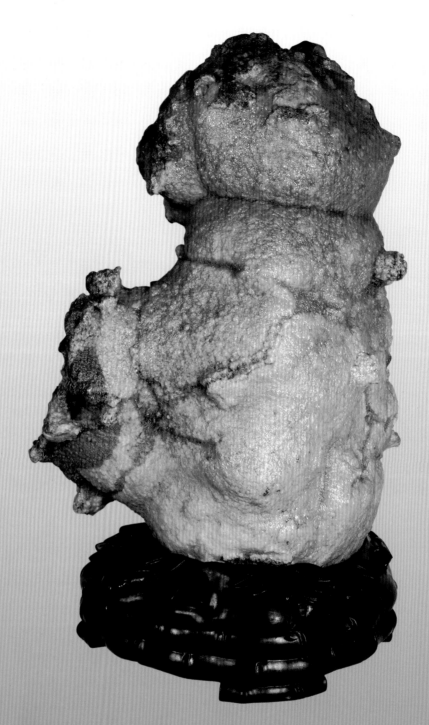

20

胖墩（沙漠漆）
Stumpy
玉髓石
42×30×23cm

少女 （沙漠漆）
Maiden
玛瑙石
11×6×5cm

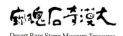
稳坐钩鱼台

Sitting calmly in a fishing boat despite the storm

红碧玉石

15×10×7cm

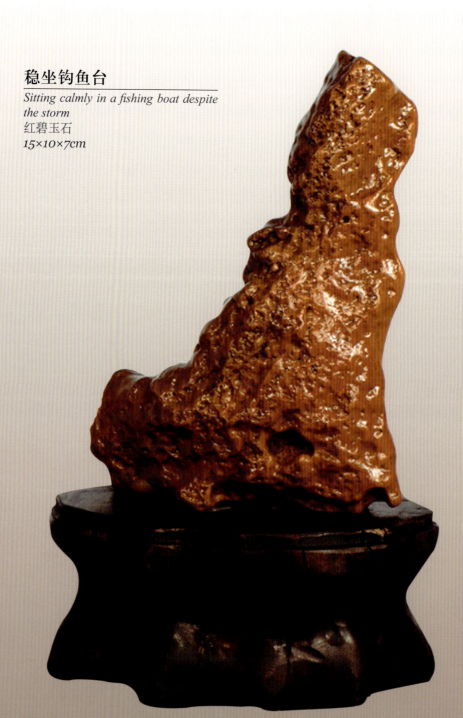

*天王

Tian Wang

巨型葡萄玛瑙玉石
108×52×40cm
约220公斤

《天王》葡萄玛瑙玉石，天生丽质、镶珠挂玉、流光溢彩，恰似累累葡萄，美仑美奂、无与伦比。极为神奇的是，他以西方广目天王仙世，万颗法珠相连，交叉成法器化法身，净观世界，护持正法，福泽大千生灵。这种罕见的智慧法像，凝聚着和谐，慈悲又庄严，色彩鲜明，形象逼真的葡萄玛瑙、珍珠玛瑙玉石，巧妙的自然组合，把广目天王因缘和合的威德展现得淋漓尽致，福禄寿尽在其中。原故宫博物院副院长杨伯达等五位国家顶级宝玉石专家一致鉴评它为国内罕见的葡萄玛瑙人像石神品！具有极高的收藏、观赏、经济和科研价值，被他们和赏石界及超百家国内外各种媒体誉为国内葡萄玛瑙第一石！

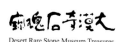

送子观音 (沙漠漆)
Jade Kwan-yin
玉髓红碧玉共生石
42×20×18cm

24

(背面)

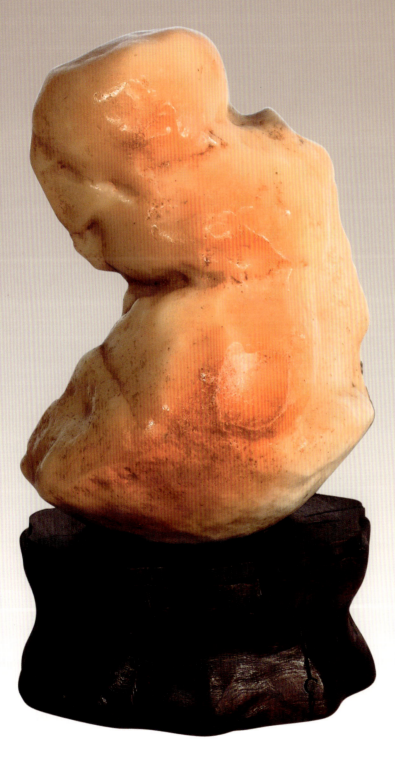

26

*恭禧发财（沙漠漆）
Congratulations for Getting Rich
财子双全
玛瑙玉髓共生石
40×16×15cm

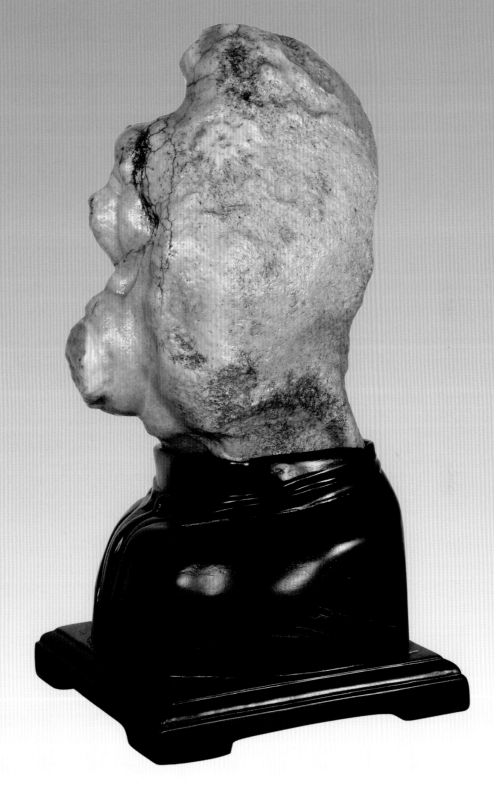

猪先生 (沙漠漆)
Mr. Pig
玉髓石
22×19×16cm

28

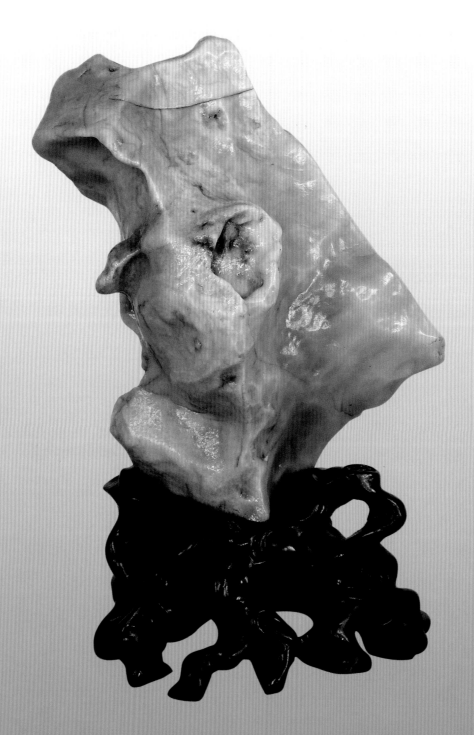

耳濡目染 (沙漠漆)
Unconscious influence by what one constantly sees or hears
玛瑙石
18×16×11cm

Desert Rare Stone Museum Treasures

*寿星姥

God of Longevity

玛瑙、红碧玉共生石

22×10×12cm

福相长寿，
是我拥有，
我拥有石德石性，
我还拥有天下石友。
别看我默默无语，
但我可使我的石友，
石来运转，与石同寿，
变得和我一样拥有。

信步（沙漠漆）
Stroll
集骨石
21×12×8cm

32

倒立（沙漠漆）
Handstand
玉髓石
20×12×11cm

钟馗 (沙漠漆)

Ghost-catcher Zhong Kui

玉髓石

72×40×40cm

背后局部

34

*博士（沙漠漆）
Doctor
红碧玉
14×17×11cm

老态龙钟（沙漠漆）
Senility
玉髓石
18×11×9cm

36

祖先（沙漠漆）
Ancestor
玉髓石
23×17×15cm

老气横秋 (沙漠漆)
Lacking in youth's vigor
玉髓石
16×12×8cm

大漠奇石瑰宝
Desert Rare Stone Museum Treasures

 象形石

看我像谁（沙漠漆）
What I look like
玉髓石
16×13×12cm

38

Desert Rare Stone Museum Treasures
象形石

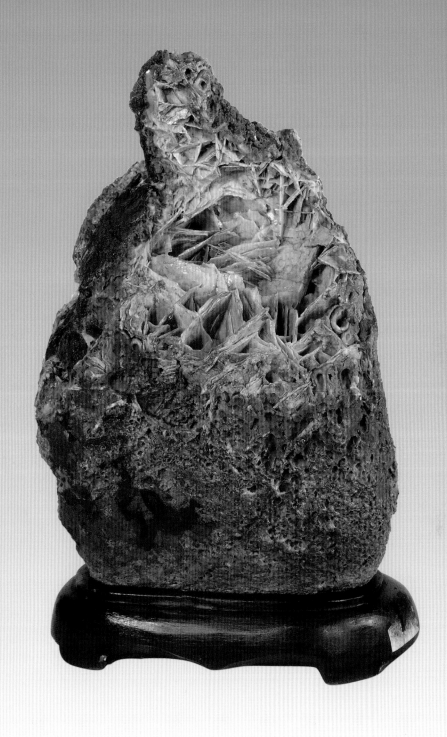

胸有成竹（沙漠漆）
Have a thought-out plan
集骨玛瑙石
31×21×20cm

40

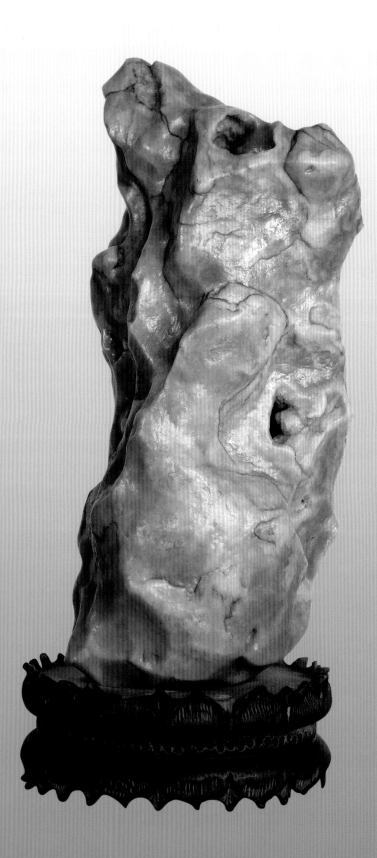

闭关修炼 (沙漠漆)
Close-door Exercise
玉髓石
23×10×11cm

慧眼识珠（沙漠漆）

Sharp Insight
玉髓石
36×38×35cm

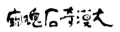

42

*山姆

uncleSam

多色玛瑙玉石

28×16×15cm

《山姆》奇石形成于二亿年前的火山喷发，其肉色皮肤、棕色眼睛、高高的鼻子翘嘴巴以及棕色的头发，严然一位活生生的山姆大叔！就人类进化史而言，这位北美"先人"在二亿年前由火山爆发就一步到位，您说他有多神奇！此石是典型的人物象形石，其头型、五官、神态以至脖子、脖筋都十分逼真。因此，原故宫博物院副院长杨伯达等五位国家顶级宝玉石专家一致鉴评它是神在天成，奇在自然的玛瑙玉石中不可多得的天然而成的人物具像石极品！

希腊人（沙漠漆）
Greek
集骨石
28×23×14cm

44

非洲少女 (沙漠漆)
African Maiden
灰玛瑙石
39×25×11cm

桂冠 (沙漠漆)
Crown
玉髓石
38×27×25cm

46

外星人（沙漠漆）
E. T.
集骨石
15×14×13cm

非洲先生（沙漠漆）
Mr. Africa
玛瑙玉髓共生石
33×25×15cm

48

狂吻（沙漠漆）
Wild Kiss
玉髓石
18×15×10cm

*绅士 (沙漠漆)
Gentlemna
红碧玉
14×17×11cm

50

期盼平安归
Expecting safe return
玉髓石
14×23×12cm

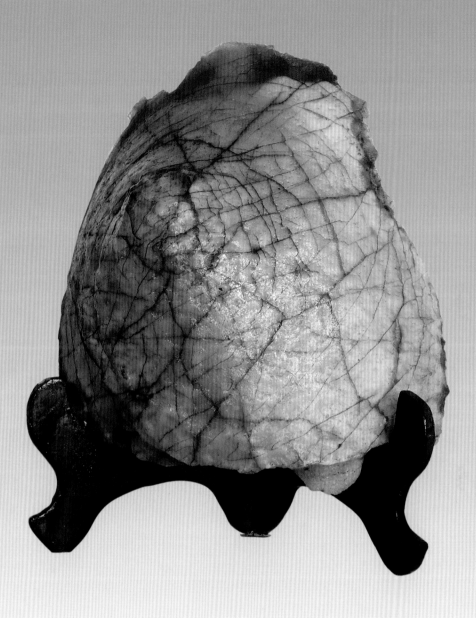

母韵 (沙漠漆)
Mother's Charm
玛瑙石
21×18×9cm

昭君出塞（沙漠漆）
The princess of "zhao jun"
玛瑙石
16×10×6cm

52

羞（沙漠漆）
Expecting safe return
玉髓石
31×18×10cm

54

父子情 (沙漠漆)
Father and Son
玉髓石
48×30×35cm

门之艺术 (沙漠漆)

Art of Door

玛瑙玉髓共生石

45×33×32cm

56

傲慢（沙漠漆）
Arrogance
玉髓石
26×16×15cm

（背面）

*圣僧
Saint Monk
葡萄玛瑙石
41×20×16cm

大漠奇石館
Desert Rare Stone Museum Treasures

象形石

58

沙漠之王（沙漠漆）
King of Desert
玉髓石
32×31×25cm

大漠奇石館
Desert Rare Stone Museum Treasures

象形石

猪首 （沙漠漆）
Pig Head
玛瑙玉髓共生石
28×21×25cm

热恋（沙漠漆）
Sweet Love
玛瑙玉髓共生石
15×11×5cm

60

马首 (沙漠漆)

Horse Head

玉髓石

31×21×18cm

62

松狮 (沙漠漆)
Chow Chow
玉髓石
62×52×18cm

64

等待
Wait
绿碧玉石
29×18×13cm

*小八戒（沙漠漆）
Piglet
灰玛瑙
15×13×9cm

66

翼龙
Pterosaur
玉髓石
29×25×24cm

（背面）

神气银狐
Magical Silver Fox
玛瑙石
16×10×17cm

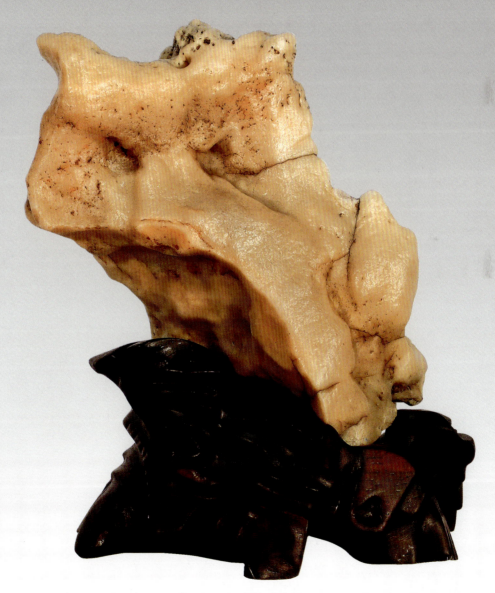

68

蛇首（沙漠漆）
Snake Head
玉髓石
19×15×9cm

虎仔（沙漠漆）

Young Tiger

玉髓石

21×14×11cm

（背面）

70

春情 (沙漠漆)
Spring Emotion
彩色玛瑙石
16×23×8cm

恐龙 (沙漠漆)
Dinosaur
玛瑙石
19×11×9cm

72

声嘶力竭 (沙漠漆)
Shout Hoarse
玉髓石
22×11×10cm

74

*母子情（沙漠漆）
Motherhoood
玛瑙玉髓组合
22×22×16cm

金蛙鸣曲（沙漠漆）
Croak
玛瑙石
16×14×7cm

（背面）

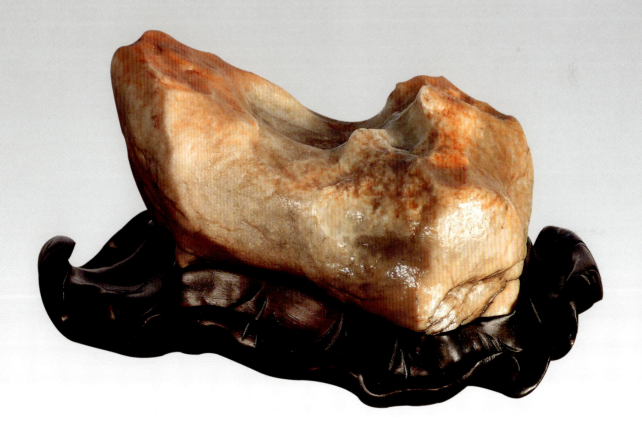

76

鱼乐图
Fishing
玛瑙石
19×16×6cm

母以子贵 （沙漠漆）

Mother is Prized Because of Her Son

玉髓石

36×29×25cm

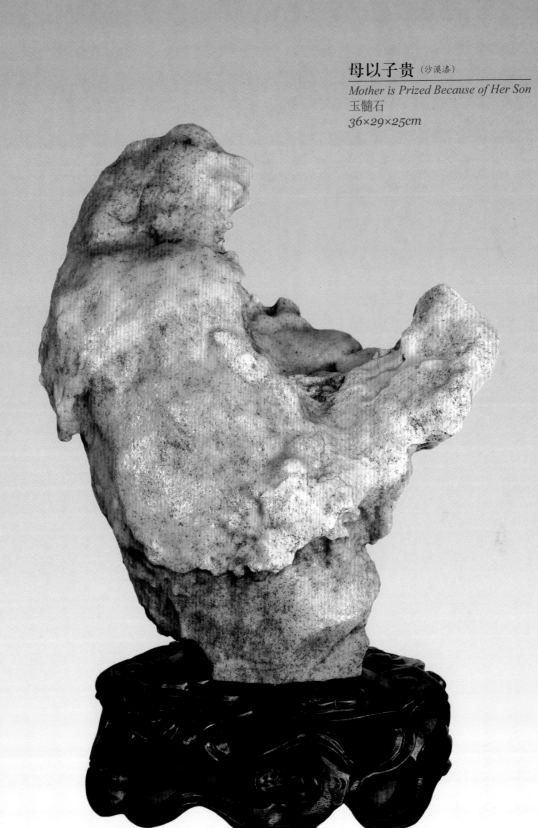

78

忍者神龟（沙漠漆）
Devine Tortoise
玉髓石
17×13×6cm

富贵金猪 <small>(沙漠漆)</small>
Fortune Gold Pig
玉髓石
61×32×18cm

80

象山（沙漠漆）
Elephant Mountain
玉髓石
40×33×32cm

龙骨 (沙漠漆)
Dragon Bone
玉髓石
25×18×16cm

熊样（沙漠漆）
Bear-like
玉髓石
28×23×20cm

82

猪娃（沙漠漆）
Pig Baby
玉髓石
35×22×19cm

怯
Fear
玉髓石
19×14×12cm

84

*独霸

Monopolization

葡萄玛瑙石

22×23×12cm

大漠奇石馆
Desert Rare Stone Museum Treasures

象形石

86

守猎 (沙漠漆)
Hunting
玉髓石
49×35×21cm

吾面何方（沙漠漆）

Which direction I am facing

玉髓石

32×30×25cm

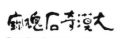
88

目瞪口呆（沙漠漆）

Stunned and Speechless

玉髓石

29×25×15cm

（背面）

神气十足（沙漠漆）

Vigorous

玉髓石

21×18×13cm

90

雄鸡（沙漠漆）
Rooster
集骨玛瑙玉髓共生石
35×32×23cm

92

金狐狸（沙漠漆）
Golden Fox
玉髓石
30×20×15cm

与世无争 (沙漠漆)

Stand aloof from worldly affairs

玉髓石

28×19×15cm

94

*母子情

Motherhoood

玛瑙碧玉共生石

20×18×15cm

初为鸽母心中喜，幼小娇儿背上依。
愿子随父碧空尽，和平使者播信息。

静观其变 (沙漠漆)
Wait and See
玉髓石
63×56×28cm

96

宁静致远（沙漠漆）

Tranquility

玉髓石

52×31×19cm

（背面）

大漠奇石瑰宝

Desert Rare Stone Museum Treasures

98

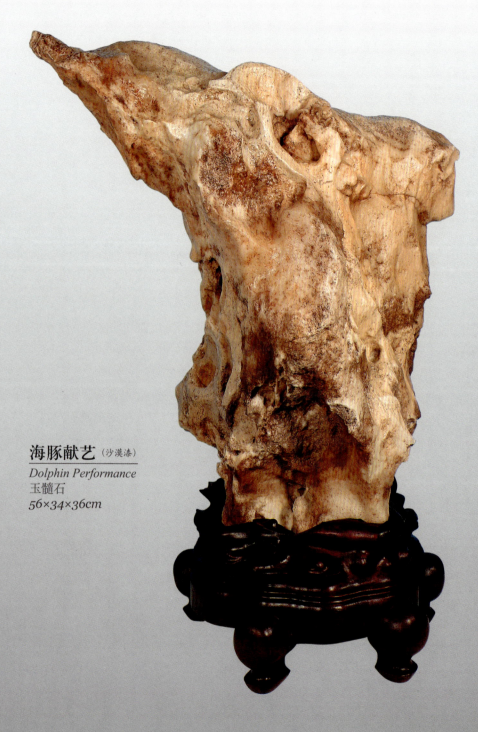

海豚献艺（沙漠漆）
Dolphin Performance
玉髓石
56×34×36cm

刺瑰石寺漢大
Desert Rare Stone Museum Treasures

海狮 (沙漠漆)
Sea Lion
玉髓石
22×17×13cm

100

健美
Beauty and Strength
玉髓石
32×31×16cm

回首（沙漠漆）
Look Back
玉髓石
20×11×11cm

（背面）

大漠奇石瑰宝
Desert Rare Stone Museum Treasures

102

蝶之舞（沙漠漆）
Dance of Butterfly
玉髓石
44×36×20cm

相视无语

Look at each other without words

玉髓石

35×30×22cm

104

俯视
Look Down
玉髓石
37×23×18cm

*沙皮狗
Sharpei Dog
玛瑙石
19×17×14cm

大漠奇石馆藏
Desert Rare Stone Museum Treasures

106

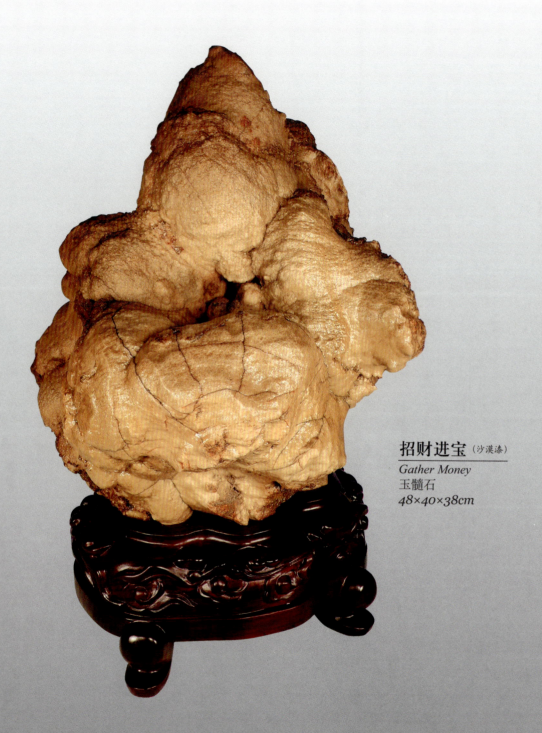

招财进宝（沙漠漆）
Gather Money
玉髓石
48×40×38cm

火焰山 (沙漠漆)
Volcano Land
玉髓石
45×42×24cm

108

手舞足蹈 (沙漠漆)
Flourish
玉髓石
39×40×19cm

金虎（沙漠漆）
Golden Tiger
玉髓石
35×28×17cm

蝴蝶石寺漢大
Desert Rare Stone Museum Treasures

110

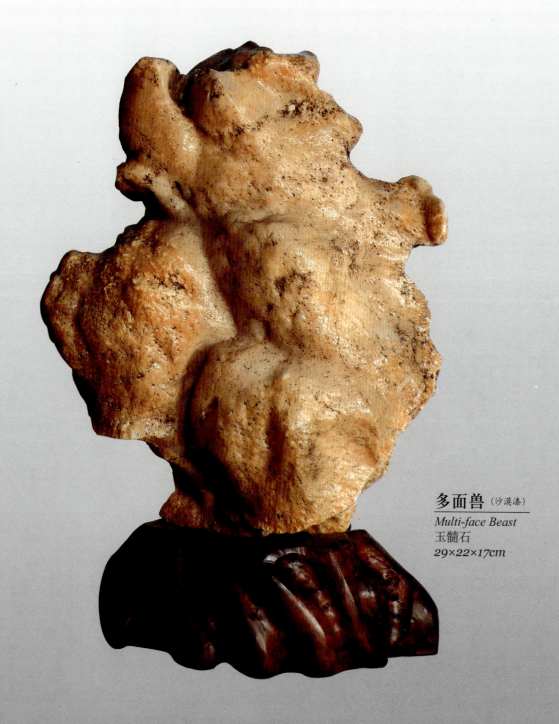

多面兽（沙漠漆）
Multi-face Beast
玉髓石
29×22×17cm

穿山甲 (沙漠漆)

Pangolin

玉髓石

26×24×20cm

*永不凋谢的花
Non-withered Flower
红碧玉玛瑙共生石
18×12×6cm

112

回眸 （沙漠漆）
Turning the head
玉髓石
21×16×10cm

大漠奇石瑰
Desert Rare Stone Museum Treasures

114

多春
Spring
红葡萄玛瑙石
32×22×9cm

大漠奇石瑰
Desert Rare Stone Museum Treasures

恕

Forgive
玛瑙玉髓共生石
31×21×22cm

116

小憩
Catnap
玉髓石
32×26×15cm

118

供
Supply
玛瑙玉髓共生石
_12×16×19cm_

负重 （沙漠漆）

Load

玉髓石

21×16×12cm

120

*刺猬 （沙漠漆）
Hedgehog
玛瑙碧玉共生石
16×18×11cm

十月怀胎 (沙漠漆)
Pregnant
玉髓石
23×21×7cm

 象形石

狮子（沙漠漆）
Lion
玉髓石
22×14×9cm

122

大漠奇石馆藏
Desert Rare Stone Museum Treasures

虎头虎脑 (沙漠漆)
Lovely and Energetic
玉髓石
30×29×26cm

124

洗耳恭听（沙漠漆）
All Ears
玉髓石
28×20×12cm

闭目养神 (沙漠漆)
Repose with eyes closed
玉髓石
20×16×12cm

126

鞠躬尽瘁（沙漠漆）
Spare no effort
玉髓石
23×18×12cm

128

趾高气扬 （沙漠漆）
Hold one's head high
玉髓石
34×23×17cm

猿头化石
Ape Head Fossil
玉髓石
21×16×15cm

130

东方醒狮

The East awakes the lion
葡萄玛瑙石
16×23×6cm

志在千里
(立面)

外柔内刚 (沙漠漆)

Outwardly soft and inwardly hard

玉髓石

17×14×13cm

132

自得其乐（沙漠漆）
Being content with one's lot
玉髓石
60×36×28cm

海底称雄 (沙漠漆)

Rule the sea floor

玉髓石

52×35×23cm

134

狮子王 (沙漠漆)
Lion King
玉髓石
13×17×11cm

心不在焉 (沙漠漆)
Absent-minded
玉髓石
23×15×11cm

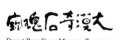

136

刺猬（沙漠漆）
Hedgehog
玉髓石
16×13×10cm

138

高瞻远瞩（沙漠漆）
Great Foresight
玉髓石
17×14×9cm

*冲天吼
Big Mouth
绿碧玉
18×17×12cm

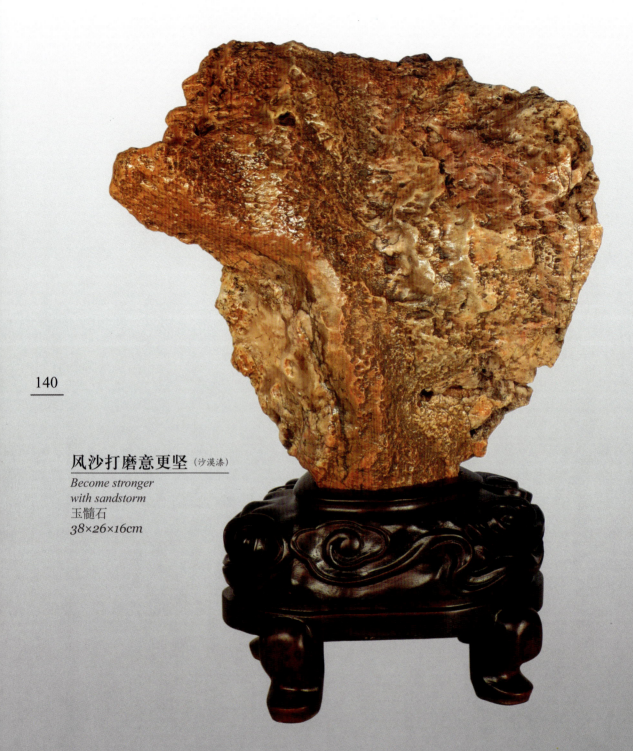

140

风沙打磨意更坚 (沙漠漆)
*Become stronger
with sandstorm*
玉髓石
38×26×16cm

京巴 （沙漠漆）
Beijing Retriever
玉髓石
25×17×12cm

贵夫犬（沙漠漆）
Poodle
玉髓石
40×32×70cm

142

年迈鸡婆 (沙漠漆)
Aged Granny
集骨玛瑙玉髓共生石
29×19×12cm

Desert Rare Stone Museum Treasures

 象形石

144

*珍珠鸡 (沙漠漆)
Guinea fowl
葡萄玛瑙石
19×17×12cm

耐心（沙漠漆）
Patience
玉髓石
37×59×31cm

146

卧佛（沙漠漆）
Reclined Buddha
玉髓石
62×68×46cm

耐人寻味（沙漠漆）

Affording for Tnoughts

玉髓石

46×57×36cm

大漠奇石珍藏
Desert Rare Stone Museum Treasures

148

寿桃（沙漠漆）
Peach shaped birthday cake
玉髓石
43×60×40cm

景观 静物石

Landscape & Static Image Chapter

150

千年等一回（沙漠漆）
Waiting for once in one thousand years
玉髓石
35×23×12cm

双乳峰 (沙漠漆)
Breast Hills
玉髓石
25×20×19cm

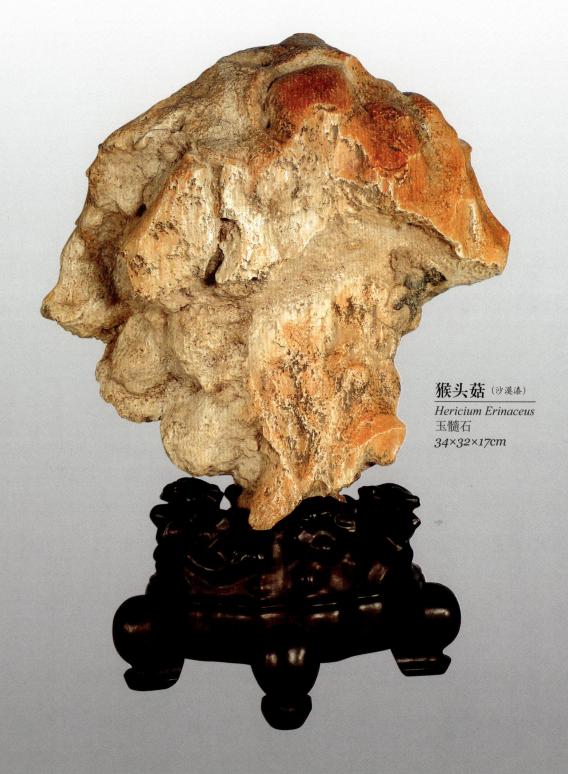

152

猴头菇（沙漠漆）
Hericium Erinaceus
玉髓石
34×32×17cm

编织岁月
Weave Years
集骨石
58×48×28cm

154

*千古栈道
Immortal Plank Road Built along a Cliff
玛瑙千层共生石
28×35×16cm
征履栈道险，残云奇峰间。
硝烟兵戟骨，相传又几千。

156

火痕
Fire Trace
玛瑙玉髓共生石
38×35×28cm

仁者乐山

The Virtuous Find Pleasure in Hills

玉髓石

48×44×35cm

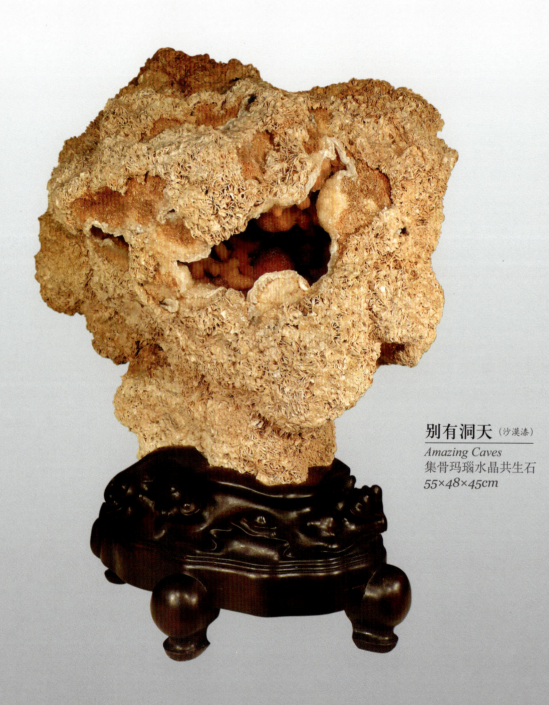

158

别有洞天 (沙漠漆)
Amazing Caves
集骨玛瑙水晶共生石
55×48×45cm

山神 (沙漠漆)
Fairyland
玉髓石
30×28×25cm

（背面）

160

网络
Mountain God
集骨石
38×35×35cm

晚霞如染 (沙漠漆)
Network
玉髓石
23×18×6cm

162

爱不释手（沙漠漆）
Red Sunglow
玉髓石
23×21×17cm

*掌上明珠
Glittering jade beads
葡萄玛瑙石
30×52×16cm

164

景观 静物石

石破天惊 (沙漠漆)
Flying Gold on Palace
玉髓玛瑙共生石
30×28×22cm

166

叠翠（沙漠漆）

Green Peaks Over Peaks

玉髓石

53×46×36cm

石破天惊（沙漠漆）
Remarkably original and forceful
玛瑙石
82×75×40cm

168

堆靠 (沙漠漆)
Piles
玛瑙玉髓共生石
40×35×30cm

红艳欲滴（沙漠漆）
Bright Red
玉髓石
29×25×13cm

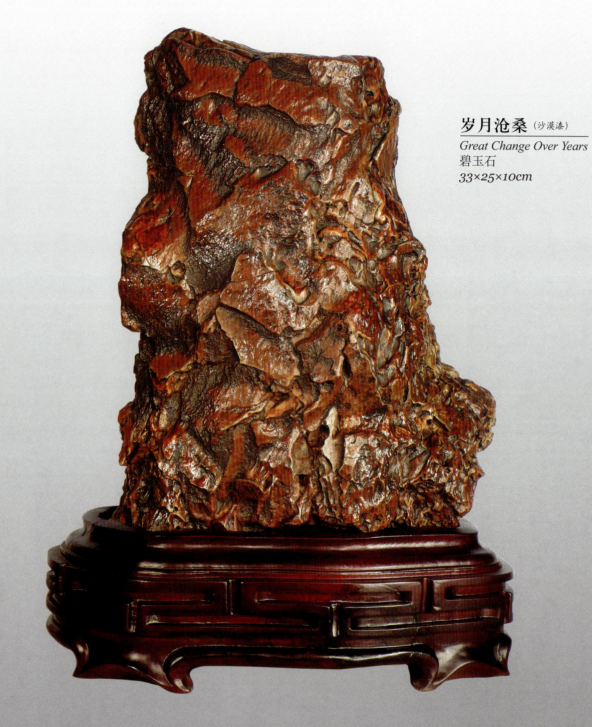

岁月沧桑 (沙漠漆)
Great Change Over Years
碧玉石
33×25×10cm

170

（背面）

菊颂

Chrysanthemum Ode

集骨玛瑙石

42×30×18cm

172

麦桔山 (沙漠漆)

Cornstock Hills

集骨玉髓共生石

32×23×19cm

(背面)

珠光宝气（沙漠漆）
Precious and Extraordinary
集骨玉髓水晶共生石
31×26×23cm

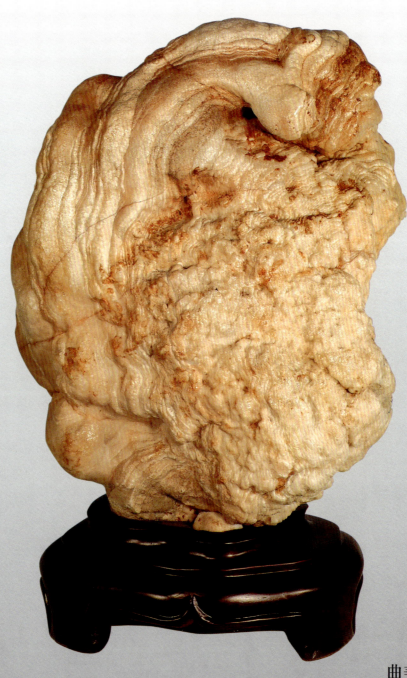

174

曲美（沙漠漆）

Curved Beauty

玛瑙玉髓共生石

32×25×21cm

張力

Tension

集骨石

42×33×25cm

*奥秘之珠
Pearly of Mystery
葡萄玛瑙石
38×18×16cm

176

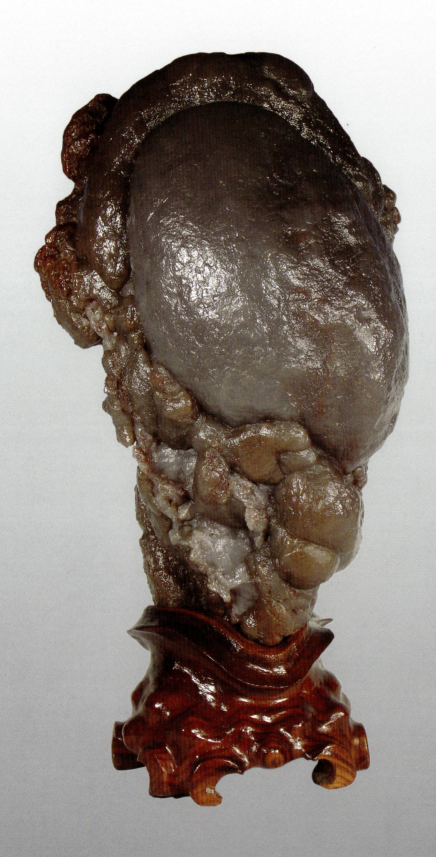

金鱼山（沙漠漆）
Goldfish Hill
玉髓石
48×32×22cm

178

黄氏山水 (沙漠漆)
Huang Shi Mountains and Rivers
玉髓石
35×32×30cm

金砖（沙漠漆）
Gold Brick
玉髓石
38×17×11cm

180

精镂细刻 (沙漠漆)
Delicate Carving
集骨玛瑙石
28×25×23cm

鬼斧神功

Nature's marvel

玛瑙石

47×34×18cm

182

红红火火 (沙漠漆)
Prosperous
玉髓石
35×31×13cm

184

华丽美观 (沙漠漆)
Magnificent and Wonderful
玛瑙玉髓共生石
22×20×17cm

霜叶红于二月花 (沙漠漆)
Maple Leaves as Red as February Flowers
玉髓石
29×25×24cm

186

双峰争秀 (沙漠漆)
Elegant Double-peak
玉髓石
32×26×22cm

蟒山 （沙漠漆）
Python mountain
玉髓石
30×29×18cm

188

水晶宫
Crystal Palace
玛瑙水晶玉髓共生石
45×35×26cm

润 (沙漠漆)

Smootha
玛瑙玉髓共生石
29×26×21cm

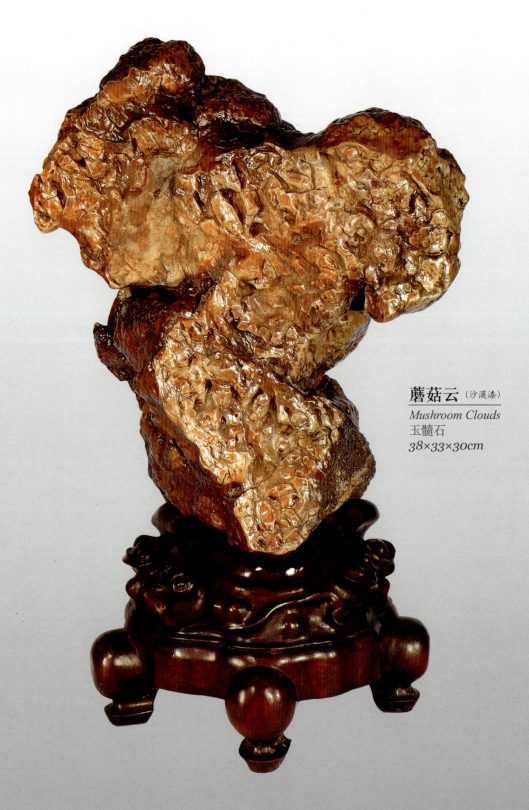

190

蘑菇云（沙漠漆）
Mushroom Clouds
玉髓石
38×33×30cm

金壁辉煌（沙漠漆）
Splendid in Green and Gold
玉髓石
52×36×18cm

192

日出（沙漠漆）
Sunrise
碧玉石
45×34×25cm

火烧赤壁（沙漠漆）
Chibi on Fire
玉髓石
39×26×13cm

194

青面獠牙

Green face and ferocious fangs

玛瑙石

16×14×12cm

云台山（沙漠漆）
Yuntai Mountain
玉髓石
27×26×2cm

遨游太空（沙漠漆）
Travel over space
玉髓石
17×15×14cm

196

*自然天成
The natural day becomes
黑碧玉石
27×22×16cm

198

红霞映山（沙漠漆）
Red sunglow reflects on hills
玉髓石
48×31×29cm

200

艳丽悦目 (沙漠漆)
Gorgeous Beauty
灰玛瑙石
44×38×32cm

202

魂系大漠 (沙漠漆)
Soul of Desert
玉髓石
47×27×28cm

隔山望月（沙漠漆）
Enjoy moonlight over hills
玉髓石
31×28×21cm

204

钢筋铁骨（沙漠漆）
Iron Bones
玉髓石
26×26×25cm

秋韵 (沙漠漆)

Charm of Autumn

玉髓石

44×30×28cm

206

春恋 (沙漠漆)
Love of Spring
玉髓石
21×15×6cm

（局部）

大珠小珠落玉盘（沙漠漆）
Big and small drops onto jade plate
玉髓水晶共生石
99×65×68cm

208

金屋 （沙漠漆）
Gold House
玉髓石
21×20×16cm

仙人洞（沙漠漆）
Fairy Cave
玉髓石
38×30×31cm

210

海底世界（沙漠漆）
Seabed World
玉髓石
26×16×15cm

黄金甲（沙漠漆）
Gold Armor
玉髓石
28×20×15cm

212

影子 (沙漠漆)
Shade
玉髓水晶共生石
28×22×23cm

玉衣
Jade Clothes
集骨石
50×35×32cm

山川秀丽 (沙漠漆)
Elegant hills and plains
玛瑙玉髓共生石
43×35×18cm

214

（另面）

国画
Traditional Chinese Painting
玛瑙水晶共生石
25×19×15cm

216

远山滴翠（沙漠漆）
Green Mountains
彩色玛瑙石
30×20×18cm

美味（沙漠漆）
Delicacy
玛瑙玉髓共生石
19×10×9cm

218

锦上添花（沙漠漆）
Flowers and Cheers
集骨石
30×26×21cm

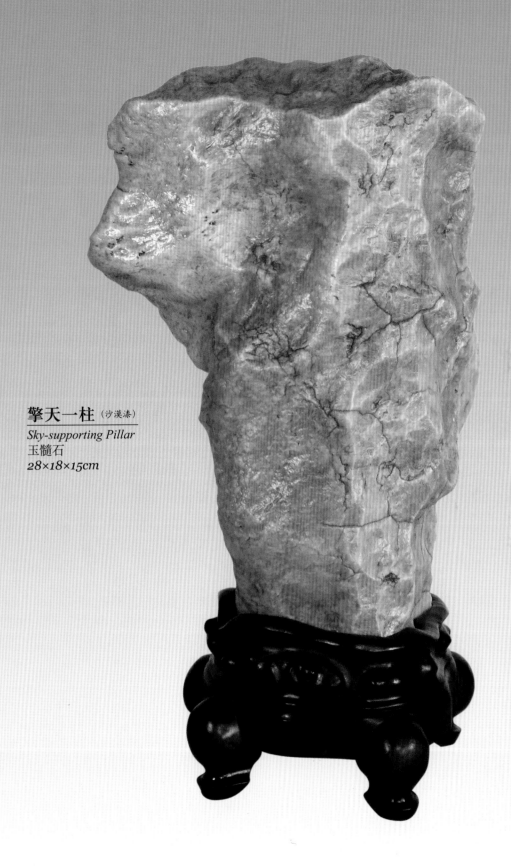

擎天一柱 (沙漠漆)
Sky-supporting Pillar
玉髓石
28×18×15cm

220

玉花
Jade Flower
集骨石
24×18×12cm

金镶玉 (沙漠漆)

Gold inlaid with jade

玉髓石

27×23×22cm

222

万山红遍 (沙漠漆)
Red Mountains
玉髓石
32×20×20cm

金冠（沙漠漆）

Gold crown

玉髓石

32×28×29cm

224

斗艳（沙漠漆）
Fights colorfully
玉髓石
28×23×16cm

晚霞如染（沙漠漆）
The sunset glow like dyes
集骨玛瑙玉髓共生石
35×22×21cm

226

点石成金（沙漠漆）

Touching a stone and turn it into gold

玉髓石

26×25×22cm

（背面）

小家子气 （沙漠漆）
Pettiness
玉髓石
38×56×31cm

228

梦笔生花 (沙漠漆)

The dream pen lives the flower

集骨玉髓共生石

38×76×31cm

（侧面）

紫花
Red indigo
水晶玉髓共生石
28×39×16cm

230

人间天彩 (沙漠漆)
Colo rful Sky
玉髓石
31×32×26cm

后记

　　大漠奇石馆建成已经五年了，接待了不少游客和朋友，还有新闻界的报导和宣传，使大家都知道昌平流村的大漠奇石馆，我也因是石馆的主人出了"名"，但我心里并无惬意，总觉得对不住这些奇石。一是没有配过象样的底座，还是十年前的老样子；二是没有从石堆里挑选一些新品展现给石友们，还是那些老面孔；三是没出过一本像样的书，让更多的读者来了解大漠石，弘扬石文化。

　　如今好了，经过一年多的准备工作，把原来的旧座换成了红木座，又从石堆里选出了一些没有开发过的奇石，共整理出200余方精品。在昌平区委、区政府领导的亲切关怀下，昌平旅游局、昌平区科协、流村镇政府大力支持下，出版发行了这册《大漠奇石瑰宝》展现给石友们。

　　我平生喜欢书画艺术，更爱奇石、特别是大漠石。从与大漠石相识那一刻起，十余年就没有分开过，至今相爱如初。是奇石的魅力，还是我的偏爱，说不清楚，也许是"缘分"吧，就像聂卫平说的"如果你学会了下围棋，那么你一生就离不开围棋。"一样。如今我已花甲之年，仍痴心不改，看着这些精美奇石，还那么兴奋，那么激动，从无厌之感。有时从石堆翻出一方精品如获至宝，高兴好一阵子，赏石给我带来健康、带来愉悦，石头是自然的，人也是自然的，人与石交往是和谐的。

　　在《大漠奇石瑰宝》出版之即，向多年来给予奇石馆大力支持的昌平区委、区政府，昌平旅游局、区科协、流村镇政府、古将村人民表示感谢。向多年来关心和帮助过的侯一民老先生、蓝天野老先生、欧阳中石老先生、张靖老先生、赵立云先生表示深厚的谢意。

　　希望广大石友对本书的不足之处给予指正。

2008年6月28日

Desert Rare Stone Museum Treasures

Postscript

It has been 5 years since the founding of Desert Rare Stone Museum. During this period, we've received numerous visitors and guests. Thanks to the reports and promotion by the media, our museum in Liucun Town of Changping District became well-known to all and I also won a good fame as the host. However, I didn't feel pleased at all. Instead I was sorry to the rare stones, for which there are three reasons: first, the base is still left what it was ten years ago; second, there are few new exhibits in the museum; and third, I failed to come up with a good book to help more readers better understand the desert stones as well as stone culture.

Now everything changes for the better. After over a year's preparation, the old base has been replaced with a new red one. A bunch of undeveloped rare stones have been selected from the stone piles and more than 200 exquisite stones sorted out. Under the concern of Changping government leadership and with the great support of Changping Tourism Bureau, Changping Scientific Association and Liucun Town government, I was able to publish this "Desert Rare Stone Treasures" to extensive stone lovers.

I have been enjoying paintings and calligraphy all my life, and I prefer rare stones especially desert stones. Ever since I first saw them, I have never parted with them and have kept a deep affection for them as before. It is hard to tell whether it's due to my preference or because of the so-called "chemical". Just as Nie Weiping once said, "If you have learnt how to play chess, you cannot live without it." I am now 60 years old, but still addicted to these fantastic rare stones, with no less excitement than before. I never feel bored with them. Sometimes when I find an exquisite stone from the piles I'll be happy for a long time.

2008.6.28